THE MAKE-SOMETHING CLUB

Winky

Skipper

Tag

THE MAKE-SOMETHING CLUB

FUN WITH CRAFTS, FOOD, AND GIFTS

By Frances Zweifel

Illustrated by Ann Schweninger

PUFFIN BOOKS

This book is dedicated to all the patient and loving people
who take the time to help children discover
the lifelong pleasures of making things with their own hands.
—F. Z.

For Deborah Brodie
—A. S.

The art was prepared with graphite pencil,
color pencil, and watercolor paint on
Fabriano 90-pound cold-press watercolor paper.

PUFFIN BOOKS
Published by the Penguin Group
Penguin Books USA Inc., 375 Hudson Street, New York, New York 10014, U.S.A.
Penguin Books Ltd, 27 Wrights Lane, London W8 5TZ, England
Penguin Books Australia Ltd, Ringwood, Victoria, Australia
Penguin Books Canada Ltd, 10 Alcorn Avenue, Toronto, Ontario, Canada M4V 3B2
Penguin Books (N.Z.) Ltd, 182–190 Wairau Road, Auckland 10, New Zealand
Penguin Books Ltd, Registered Offices: Harmondsworth, Middlesex, England

First published in the United States of America by Viking,
a division of Penguin Books USA Inc., 1994
Simultaneously published in Puffin Books

3 5 7 9 10 8 6 4 2

Text copyright © Frances Zweifel, 1994
Illustrations copyright © Ann Schweninger, 1994
All rights reserved

LIBRARY OF CONGRESS HAS CATALOGUED THE VIKING EDITION AS FOLLOWS:
Zweifel, Frances W.
The make-something club/by Frances Zweifel; illustrated by Ann Schweninger.
p.   cm.
Summary: A how-to guide for projects such as making pine cone bird-feeders,
frog sock puppets, pasta necklaces, and a variety of snacks and desserts.
ISBN 0-670-82361-9
[1. Handicraft—Juvenile literature.   2. Cookery—Juvenile literature.
[1. Handicraft.   2. Cookery.]   I. Schweninger, Ann, ill.   II. Title.
TT160.Z39   1994   745.5—dc20   93-2393   CIP   AC

Puffin Books ISBN 0-14-050741-8
Printed in Hong Kong

CONTENTS

Introducing Winky, Skipper, and Tag

Something for a Snack

I'm hungry. Can we make something to eat?

Let's make some Polka-dot Toast.

Polka-dot Toast

Ingredients: 1 slice of bread for each child, cream cheese, raisins

Materials: plate, table knife, tablespoon

Directions:

1. Toast a slice of bread for each snacker.

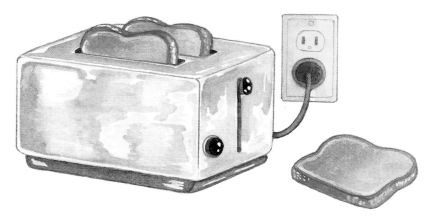

2. Spread each piece of warm toast with cream cheese.

3. Sprinkle about 1 tablespoon raisins on each piece.

4. Press the raisins lightly into the cream cheese.

Suggestion: You can use currants or chopped dates or apricots in place of raisins.

Polka-dot Toast

FEBRUARY

Something for the Birds

Pinecone Bird Feeders

Ingredients: peanut butter, birdseed

Materials: several large pinecones, wax paper, table knife, string, scissors

Directions:

1. Cut a length of string 1 to 2 feet long.

2. Tie the string around a pinecone near the top, so the cone hangs down.

3. Spread out a sheet of wax paper. Hold the cone down on the wax paper. Spread peanut butter all over the cone.

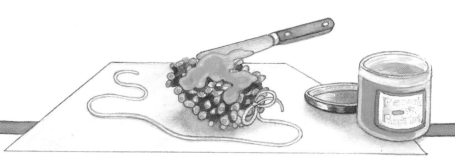

4. Sprinkle birdseed over the cone.

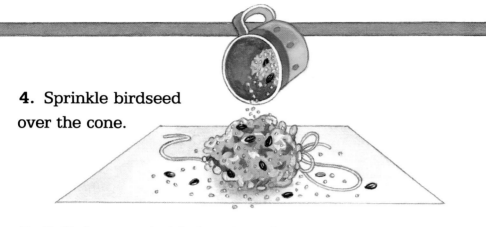

5. Roll the cone in birdseed on the wax paper. Repeat with the rest of the cones.

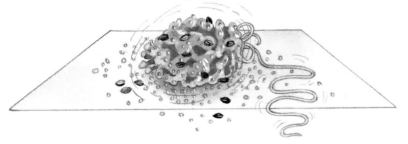

6. Tie the cones to tree branches.

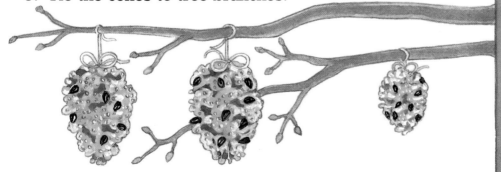

Suggestion: No birdseed? Use dry oatmeal or cornmeal.

Pinecone Bird Feeder

Something to Play With

Let's make something to play with.

Puppets are fun and they can talk to you.

Frog Sock Puppet

Materials: cotton balls or facial tissues, short pieces of string or rubber bands, scissors, black felt-tip marker, an old child-sized sock (green, if possible) for each puppet

Directions:

1. Squeeze three cotton balls or a facial tissue into a tight wad.

2. Stuff this into one side of the toe of a sock, to make an eye for the frog.

3. Cut a short piece of string, about 6 inches long. Tie the string tightly around the bottom of the bulge to hold the "eye" in place on the sock, or use a rubber band.

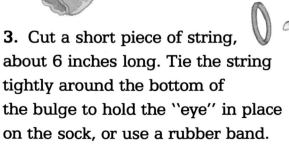

4. Repeat for the frog's other eye.

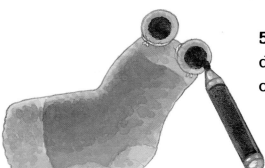

5. With the marker, draw a large pupil on each eye.

6. To work the puppet, put one hand inside the sock with your fingers in the toe and your thumb in the heel. Open and close the hand to make the puppet "talk."

Hint: If the head looks too flat, stuff a wad of paper towel into the toe of the sock to make it rounded.

Frog
Sock
Puppet

Something for Breakfast

Breakfast Sundae

Ingredients: fruit (strawberries, sliced peaches, sliced bananas, etc.), plain or fruit-flavored yogurt, granola or other favorite cereal for topping, a pitted cherry for each sundae

Materials: cereal bowls, spoons, measuring cup, tablespoon

Directions:

1. Put about ½ cup of fruit into a bowl.

2. Pour about ¼ cup yogurt over the fruit.

3. Sprinkle on 2 or 3 tablespoons of cereal.

4. Top each sundae with a cherry.

Suggestion: You could sprinkle on raisins or shredded coconut instead of cereal.

Breakfast Sundae

Something to Wear

Pasta Necklace

Materials: string, scissors, bar of soap, uncooked colored pasta shapes with holes (such as short and long tubes and wheels)

Directions:

1. Cut a piece of string about 2 feet long.

2. Wet the soap. Stiffen one end of the string by pulling it over the soap.

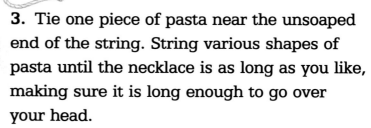

3. Tie one piece of pasta near the unsoaped end of the string. String various shapes of pasta until the necklace is as long as you like, making sure it is long enough to go over your head.

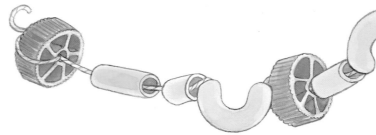

4. Tie the ends of the string together in a tight knot. Cut off the stiff end.

Suggestions: You can make a dangle in the middle of a necklace by tying off the center section in a loop. Twist two necklaces together to make a thicker necklace. Use a shorter string to make a bracelet.

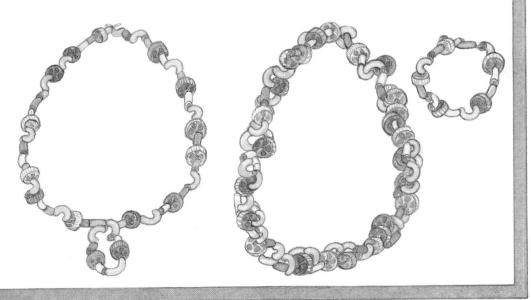

Pasta Necklace

Something to Keep

Pet Rocks

Materials: assorted smooth rocks, permanent markers, acrylic paints, water, paintbrushes, sturdy containers for mixing and thinning paints, yarn and seeds for tails and ears, scissors, glue, cardboard or paper to protect work surface

Directions:

1. Wash and dry an assortment of smooth rocks.

2. Decorate light-colored rocks with permanent markers.

3. Paint dark rocks with acrylic paint, thinned with a little water. Acrylics dry quickly; details such as eyes and noses may be added soon after the base color is applied.

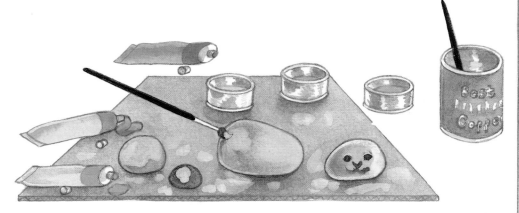

4. Allow paint to dry thoroughly before gluing on yarn tails, seed ears, etc.

Hints: To protect the work surface, cover it with newspaper or cardboard. Wash hands and brushes while the paint is still wet.

Pet Rock

JULY

Something for Lunch

Dunkers and Dips

Ingredients: "dunkers" such as carrot sticks, apple slices, breadsticks, corn chips, and bite-sized chunks of cheese; "dips" such as peanut butter thinned with milk, soft cheese spread, applesauce, and fruit yogurt

Materials: paper or plastic plates, cups for the dips, cups for milk or juice

Directions:

1. Put dunkers on a paper plate.

2. Put about ½ cup of each dip ingredient into a separate cup.

3. Put these items on a tray, or into a basket, with small cartons or cups of milk or juice. Take it all outside to eat.

Dunkers and dips for lunch is a good idea!

Pass the carrot sticks, please.

Dunkers and Dips

AUGUST

Something Growing

Bowl Garden

Materials: wide-mouth container such as a fish bowl or tank or a large jar, small trowel or large spoon for digging, gravel or pebbles, soil dug from the yard or purchased potting soil, a few small plants from garden or store, plastic wrap

Directions:

1. Wash and dry the container.

2. Put a layer of gravel or pebbles in the bottom, about an inch deep.

3. Add about 3 inches of soil. Pat the soil down.

4. Scoop a shallow well in the soil for each plant.

5. Place the plants in their wells, gently pressing the soil around the roots.

6. Slowly sprinkle on enough water to dampen the soil without washing the plants out of position.

7. Cover the container with plastic wrap, leaving a small opening at one corner.

Hints: When digging plants from the garden, try to take soil with the roots, and handle gently. Use mature plants that won't grow too tall. Place moss, pebbles, or bark bits on the soil to hold in the water and prevent drying. Check weekly for dryness. Place the bowl by a window where it will get sun part of the day.

Let's put my little glass deer in the garden.

Then we'll cover the top with plastic wrap so the garden won't dry out.

Bowl Garden

Something Pretty

Daddy and I watched falling stars last night.

Let's make some stars and hang them in our room.

We'll draw big stars and little stars.

Make a moon, too!

Silver Stars and Moon

Materials: paper plates or other thin cardboard, scissors, pencils, kitchen foil, transparent sticky tape, thread, nail or tack, star-shaped cookie cutter (if available), saucer

Directions:

1. Draw a star on a paper plate or use the cookie cutter as a guide.

2. Cut out the star.

3. Tear off a sheet of kitchen foil slightly larger around than the star.

4. Place the star on the foil. Cut the foil between the arms of the star and fold the cut edges over the arms to cover them.

5. Tape the foil down on the arms.

6. Cut a smaller piece of foil to cover the center of the star. Tape this in place.

7. With the nail or tack, poke a hole at the tip of one star arm. Tie a length of thread through the hole.

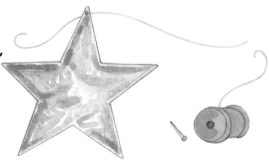

Suggestions: Make stars of different sizes. With a saucer, draw the full moon. Or draw overlapping circles with the saucer to trace a crescent shape. Cover with foil. Tape a row of stars to hang in the window or in the doorway. Or hang stars and moon from the edge of a paper plate for a mobile.

Cut
this
away

Silver Star and Moon

Something for Dessert

Apple Ghost

Ingredients: applesauce, plain or vanilla-flavored yogurt, raisins or nuts

Materials: spoons, measuring cup, mixing bowl, 3 serving bowls

Directions:

1. Measure 1 cup applesauce into the mixing bowl.

2. Add 1 cup yogurt. Stir until smooth.

3. Divide the applesauce-yogurt mixture among 3 serving bowls.

4. Place raisins or nuts on each Apple Ghost to make faces.

Suggestion: You can use whipped cream instead of yogurt.

Apple Ghost

Something Musical

Making Music

Materials: string, scissors, sticky tape, rubber bands

BELLS AND CHIMES: iron frying pan or saucepan, spoons

DRUMS: empty oatmeal box, plastic bowls with tight covers, large empty plastic bleach bottles

STRIKERS: wooden spoons, metal spoons, chopsticks

RATTLES: small plastic or metal containers with tight lids, rice or dried beans, bunch of wooden cooking utensils

Directions:

1. Make chimes by hanging a row of metal spoons from a stick or a long-handled spoon. Strike with another spoon or shake.

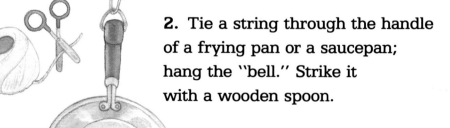

2. Tie a string through the handle of a frying pan or a saucepan; hang the "bell." Strike it with a wooden spoon.

3. Soften the sound of a striker by wrapping rubber bands around one end.

4. Put a spoonful of dry rice or beans into a rattle can; tape the top on firmly.

5. Tie the bunch of wooden utensils loosely together at their handle ends; shake them.

Suggestion: Keep time to favorite songs while singing or marching or dancing.

Musical Instruments

Something to Give

Paper Flowers

Materials: letter paper or lightweight craft paper in white or light colors, scissors, transparent sticky tape, string, ruler

Directions:

1. Starting at the short end of a sheet of letter-sized paper, fold the paper back 1 inch. Crease the fold hard.

2. Turn the paper over and fold it back another inch, exactly on top of the first fold. Crease it hard.

3. Keep on folding back and forth, like an accordion, until you have a long strip of folds.

4. Fold this strip end to end, to mark the middle. Unfold, and cut out a tiny V on both sides of the center mark—but don't cut through the center.

5. Cut the ends of the folded strip into points. Cut out 2 or 3 small V's along both sides of the strip.

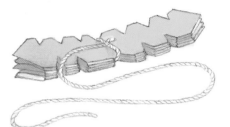

6. Cut a piece of string about 12 inches long. Tie one end tightly around the middle of the strip.

7. Fold the strip in half so the ends meet, and tape the two end petals together on the back.

8. Carefully pull the outside folds down to meet, forming a flower; tape the end petals together.

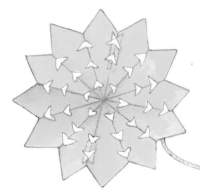

Suggestions: For smaller flowers, use half a sheet of paper; paper smaller than this is too difficult for children to handle. Tape or tack the long end of the string to a window frame so the flower dangles and catches the light in its cut-out holes. It makes a "sun-catcher."

Paper Flower

TIPS FOR MORE FUN

Safety Tips: Allow only blunt-tipped safety scissors and dull table knives for young children's projects. Chopping and slicing of ingredients should be done by an adult. Supervise the use of toasters and glass containers and the hanging of the finished crafts.

Materials: In the recipes, you may substitute your favorite ingredients for those listed. Improvise with other household items if those called for in a project are not available. For example, newspaper, especially the funnies, will make fine paper flowers; an empty cardboard box or an upturned wastepaper basket will make a dandy drum.

Adult Help: Small hands may need assistance in cutting string, tying knots, measuring ingredients, and washing up. Carrying trays of food outside may require adult help. Also, help may be needed in deciding whose turn it is to use the paint or mix the food.